C000229188

PRAYING MANTIS

CONTENTS

Front cover painting by:
D A Lish

*All photos by Russell Willis
except where indicated*

©1999 by Kingdom Books PO9 5TL ENGLAND

INTRODUCTION

The Praying Mantis has an uncanny ability to captivate all who look upon it - whether its their alien-like appearance, their haunting beauty, variety of colours and forms or their reputation as a voracious predator. One thing is for sure, these fascinating insects attract attention.

Most people are familiar with the Praying Mantis to some degree - either from an encounter on a package holiday to the Mediterranean or from seeing one in a black and white sci-fi movie (in which it is often enlarged several hundred times and is shown reaping havoc on unsuspecting space travellers). It is not surprising that the Mantis features in such films as these creatures are, without doubt, one of the most sinister looking of all insects. That disproportionately large, triangular head dominated by two giant compound eyes, a set of threatening mandibles and front legs adorned with razor sharp interlocking spines make the mantis an efficient predator. Yet their name 'Praying,' as opposed to 'Preying', belies their foreboding

An immature Malaysian Shielded Mantis in defensive pose.

nature and one wouldn't believe that those innocuous looking front legs held in their praying pose (which gives the mantis its name) are actually used for restraining prey while it is being carefully incised and eaten alive!

Another thing that sets the mantis apart from other insects is that icy cold, penetrating stare. Anyone who has seen a mantis close-up will be familiar with the way it appears to be conscious of its environment.......constantly watching. This gives one the impression that there is more to this creature than merely being an insect. It is certainly alert, appears to be calculating and is definitely unforgiving....... could the mantis be the ultimate predator?

The Praying Mantis (or Mantid) appeals to a wide range of people; whether they are intended to be a pet or a study and breeding project, mantids offer a unique insight into the fascinating natural world of insects.

Although a mantis could not be described as being a 'conventional' pet and would not take kindly to being stroked, petted or pampered, there is no reason why a mantis cannot be equally as rewarding. Watching a minute baby or nymph mantis grow up through a series of skin changes (ecdysis) and eventually become a gracious, winged adult can be very satisfying. The level of satisfaction can be increased ten-fold if the mantids that have been reared from an early age subsequently go on to breed. This is the reason why most people keep insects. Aside from their wonderful colours, shapes and interesting habits, the buzz one can obtain from rearing them through several generations makes mantis husbandry a very rewarding exercise.

One doesn't need a great deal of time, money or space to get started and mantids are not difficult to look after if a few simple ground rules are followed. In common with all animals, some species are easier to look after and breed than others and the principle aim of this book is to help the reader make an informed purchase and to serve as an introduction to the successful maintenance and breeding of these remarkable insects in captivity.

What Are Mantids?

A Praying Mantis or Mantid is an insect belonging to the order Mantodea, from a Greek word meaning 'soothsayer'.

Biologists have divided Mantodea into eight families and these are sub-divided into about 460 genera and 1800 species, although there are undoubtedly more waiting to be discovered. The eight families contained in the order are: Mantidae (the largest family); Hymenopodidae (containing the sometimes elaborately camouflaged and specialised flower mimicking species); Empusidae; Amorphoscelidae; Eremiaphilidae; Metallyticidae; Mantoididae; and Chaeteessidae. Distributed throughout the tropical, sub-tropical and temperate regions of the world, mantids occupy a wide range of habitat types ranging from lush equatorial jungle through to the dusty, dry scrubland areas of East Africa. The majority of mantid species are found in Africa followed by Asia, America and Europe, although none are found in the British Isles.

Mantids will readily drink water droplets from leaves and other terrarium decor.

BASIC ANATOMY

Unlike vertebrates, all insects have a hard outer layer to protect their internal organs. So, whilst mammals, birds and fish have bones covered in flesh (an endoskeleton), insects have an exoskeleton made from a material known as chitin.

In common with all insects, the mantid's body is divided into three main parts - the head, thorax and abdomen. These parts vary in size and shape depending on the species. Sometimes there are very significant differences in appearance between species but, under closer examination, the basic form of the insect remains the same. Some parts of the basic 'mantis model' are taken to extremes. In certain species, as a result of evolution, the result is elaborate leaf or petal-shaped bodies. Other species may have an elongated thorax that bears a close resemblance to a blade of grass or twig. At the other end of the scale, some desert dwelling species mimic small rounded pebbles and therefore have very compressed body segments. All of these adaptations afford the mantis greater protection from predators and, because mantids are not poisonous or venomous, they have to rely heavily on their camouflage in order to survive. Many species even use their camouflage to attract

African Flower Mantis (*Creobroter meleagris*) adopting a defensive posture and flashing its vivid pink wings.

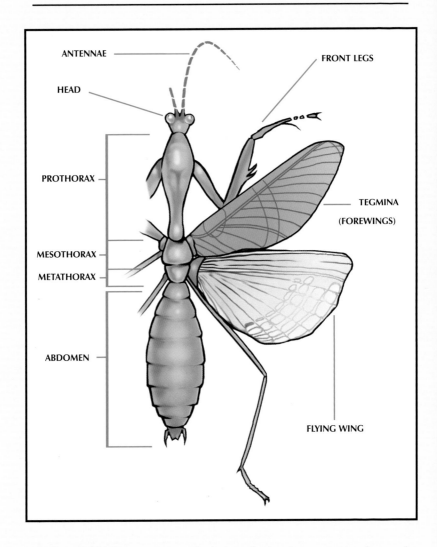

food or enable them to go unnoticed, thus allowing them a greater chance of capturing prey.

Three pairs of legs are attached to the thorax; one pair to each of the three thoracic segments, and a pair of forewings (tegmina) and a pair of flying wings (although not always capable of flight) to the second and third segments.

Attached to the first thoracic segment or prothorax is the head. This is possibly the most characteristic feature of the mantis. It is generally triangular in shape with two large and widely spaced compound eyes. Between these eyes there are often three small, simple eyes (ocelli) in a triangular formation, although they may not always be visible or present. The purpose of these eyes is not to see but to detect light and dark and alter the compound eyes accordingly.

A pair of jointed antennae are positioned on the highest point of the head between the eyes. These act as sensors, detecting changes in the environment and receiving chemical messages or pheromones which play an important part in mantis reproduction. The appearance of the antennae varies from species to species and between the sexes, males often possessing larger antennae than females. The mantis is able to rotate its head completely to either side and considerably to the rear whilst also maintaining reasonable up and down movement. This dexterity affords the mantis an excellent field of vision.

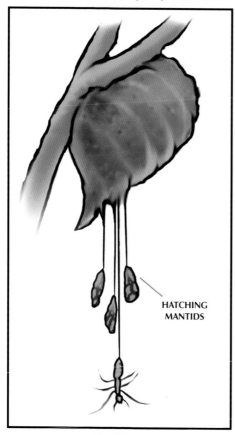

HATCHING
MANTIDS

Hatching ootheca or egg case.

Basic Mantis Anatomy (see Figure 1.)

The abdomen is softer and more flexible than other parts of the body. It is divided into eleven segments although some are reduced in size and are not clearly visible. The abdomen houses the tracheal system - the series of structures that enable the insect to breath. Air enters the insect's body through a series of small openings (spiracles) and the abdomen expands and contracts, sucking air in and expelling 'used' air from the body. The abdomen also houses the tube-like heart, gut and reproductive organs.

Obtaining A Mantis

Many pet shops now stock mantids although the range on offer may be restricted to a fairly limited number of species. Often, shops

Sometimes seen in the particularly striking pink phase, the Orchid Mantis is surely one of nature's most beautiful insects.

Pseudocreobroter whalbergi, an attractive flower mimicking species which has a limited ability to change colour, affording it a greater degree of camouflage.

OBTAINING A MANTIS

advertising reptiles for sale carry a number of interesting invertebrates or may be able to obtain them for you but be prepared to do a little shopping around. Alternatively you may have to search out a specialist entomological supplier. Quite often dealers advertise in Reptile publications or Entomological Society newsletters, details of which can be found in the Useful Addresses Section at the back of this book. If you don't happen to live near a pet shop or supplier, many companies offer a mail-order service and equipment and livestock can be delivered by courier or mail. It is also possible to purchase livefoods by mail-order.

Joining the Mantis Study group, Amateur Entomological Society or other similar societies is a good way of obtaining specimens, sharing information and meeting fellow enthusiasts. By joining a society you are taking 'pet keeping' one step further, contributing to the knowledge pool on your chosen insect and possibly aiding conservation by ensuring the captive propagation of the species (consequently reducing the number of individuals taken from the wild in order to satisfy the trade).

Do I buy a Wild-Caught or Captive-Bred mantis? The answer to this question should be clear cut: always buy Captive-Bred specimens where possible. One has to bear in mind, however, that all species will have been collected from the wild at some stage. Certain species have been bred in captivity over dozens of generations but others are relatively new to captive breeding. Imports of new species, previously unseen in the hobby, still arrive from time to time. I see no reason, providing they have been sensitively collected in small numbers and are not in any way endangered, why this should present a moral dilemma to the enthusiast. However, animals are not always sensitively collected and the shipping and housing prior to, during and after transit, often leaves a lot to be desired and one cannot condone such exploitation.

The advantages of purchasing captive bred stock in my opinion far outweigh those of buying imported specimens. Captive-bred stock is more likely to have been correctly identified, the age of the specimens is usually far easier to determine, they are likely to be parasite-free and, most importantly, one's hobby will not prove to be a drain on wild resources. On the other hand, wild-caught stock is required from time to time in order to bring fresh genetic material into captive populations and to introduce new species to culture.

SELECTING A MANTIS

It is important to select a mantis that suits your level of experience. Some species are more tolerant to unfavourable environmental conditions than others and some have quite specific requirements in captivity that need to be satisfied in order to succeed.

Due to the number of species available to the would-be enthusiast, it is impossible to describe anything other than a mere handful of species within the confines of this guide. There will always remain an element of trial and error when keeping mantids and it will be difficult to source detailed information on the species you are about to purchase. Perhaps this is one of the attractions of mantis husbandry - there is a genuine opportunity for an individual to discover something new or to perfect methods of maintenance and breeding.

The African Mantis
(*Sphodromantis lineola, centralis and viridis*)
The most commonly encountered mantis in captivity at present is the African Mantis. Several species belonging to the genus *Sphodromantis*, notably *S. lineola*, *S. centralis* and *S. viridis* are seen in the trade. However, identifying them to species level represents a bit of a challenge.

In typical praying pose, this is an African Mantis belonging to the genus *Sphodromantis*.

All these species conform to the standard mantis model and could be described as being typical in terms of shape, size and colour. The colouration of *Sphodromantis lineola* ranges from pale beige, in some individuals, through to brown or a particularly striking shade of blue green in others. Although the reason for this range of colours is likely to be genetic, as a result of geographical distribution there is some evidence to suggest that colouration may be influenced by the humidity at which the egg case or ootheca is incubated. A higher level of humidity produces a larger proportion of green hatchlings and, conversely, dry conditions produce a paler beige or brown nymph. This explanation has not, as yet, been conclusively proven.

Sphodromantis lineola reaches an adult size of approximately 8cm, the female being of slightly bulkier build than the male. Both sexes are winged and capable of flight.

Any members of the genus *Sphodromantis* represent a good first time purchase. They are particularly resilient to a wide range of environmental conditions and rarely suffer from complications during ecdysis (moulting), which can cause problems in other species. Originating from semi-arid scrubland areas they should be maintained in a dry terrarium with a relative humidity in the region of 60% and at a temperature of 75°F; a few degrees either side of this will not be detrimental to the individual.

Being hardy and prolific, they are also relatively inexpensive to purchase. If one sets out to breed this species the likelihood of rearing a large number of hatchlings to maturity is good because of the considerable size of the ootheca - several hundred hatchling nymphs may emerge from one egg case.

Madagascan Mantis (*Polyspilota aeruginosa*)

Having become increasingly available in recent years this large, robust species is another straightforward species to keep and breed. Originating in Madagascar and South East Africa and occupying a wide range of habitat types, this common species is frequently seen by road sides, in houses (where they are encouraged to eat flies) and in built-up areas.

The Madagascan Mantis is an elegant, slender species reaching about 9cm in length. Colouration ranges from brown to green. Some individuals may be of a very pale brown colour with an iridescent pearly pink hue and possess a blue/green stripe down the side of each wing case. The wings of the adult have a delicate pink tinge and slight banding of black/brown and white at the edges. There is considerable variation in the size and colour of individuals.

These large mantids are capable of attacking sizeable prey items and would have no difficulty in consuming a locust or bush cricket. Due to their aggressive nature, size and savagely spined front legs, they should be handled with care, if at all, as a stray finger is likely to be chewed as a result - this species can draw blood!

As with all mantids the size of the ootheca will vary but this species generally produces large ootheca which sometimes contain hundreds of nymphs. Given their hardiness, a breeder is likely to end up with hundreds of offspring from one successful mating. This species can be maintained in much the same way as the African *Sphodromantis* and is undemanding in its requirements.

A beautiful Madagascan Leaf Mantis. This species spends a lot of time hanging upside down, motionless amongst foliage. This individual is approximately 3 months old.

Orchid Mantis (*Hymenopus coronatus*)

Ranking among the most remarkable and intriguing of all mantids, this is a gracious creature and an evolutionary masterpiece.

Originating from the rainforests of Malaysia and the Indonesian archipelago, this angelic looking insect cunningly conceals its predatory habits in a veil of floral beauty. It perches on exotic orchids in wait of prey which comes in the form of insects visiting the flower to feed. This mantis has taken camouflage to the extreme.

Whilst the camouflage of many mantis species affords them a passing resemblance to their immediate environment, the Orchid Mantis is a convincing mimic of an orchid in its own right, although perhaps more impressive in the earlier stages of development. The delicate petal-like legs and pure white body tinged with pink, pale green and brown at the joints, a curled abdomen (in nymphs) and the position in which the mantis holds itself enable this species to occupy a somewhat specialised niche.

Occasionally one encounters the rarer and more beautiful pink phase but one should take care if purchasing a 'pink' Orchid Mantis because many pink nymphs revert to white over successive moults. As with most things, beauty has a price and the Orchid Mantis remains one of the more expensive species to buy, not least because of the patchy and unpredictable supply.

Breeding this species has always represented a challenge partly because the males and females mature at quite different rates. If a batch of nymphs is purchased often the males will be useless by the time the females eventually mature. Another problem that hampers the breeding success of this species is the general weakness of the adults having reached maturity. This can possibly be attributed to the provision of an unsuitable diet in captivity.

Given that this species mimics flowers, a large proportion of its diet will consist of pollinating/nectar feeding insects with a correspondingly high calorific value. The standard diet of captive mantids usually consists of crickets; perhaps this is unsuitable for the Orchid Mantis and a richer diet is required. Some success has been achieved feeding waxworm larvae to individuals with the help of tweezers.

Orchid Mantids require a rainforest terrarium simulating as far as possible their natural environment. This can be decorated with artificial or real plants; silk flowers are a good substitute for orchids. Relatively high humidity needs to be maintained but the air should not be allowed to stagnate; the provision of adequate ventilation should prevent this from occurring. Daily spraying with tepid water and a temperature in the region of 76-78°F is required.

The Orchid Mantis is not unusually complicated to maintain but could not be described as being one of the most hardy species. Given the high initial purchase price, it would be wise to gain experience with more tolerant species first.

African Flower Mantis (*Creobroter sp. and Pseudocreobroter sp.*)
Small, attractively marked members of these genera are being bred with increasing regularity. With a number of species sharing very similar colouration, size and habits, accurate identification is complicated. For this reason it would be wise to purchase several individuals from the same batch if breeding is to be attempted as matching up different males and females at a later date may prove difficult.

Pseudocreobroter wahlbergi is a flower mimicking species from Africa belonging to the family Hymenopodidae. These pretty little mantids are able to change colour to a certain degree to match their surroundings, although the process is not instantaneous and may take several days. In the wild they can be observed sitting on the apex of low-lying flowering plants or even on naked stems where they could easily be mistaken for a bloom by pollinating insects. Though not great in stature, these bold mantids will tackle surprisingly large prey and their agility enables them to capture fast moving and even flying insects.

As previously mentioned, a large number of species over a wide distribution

A female African Flower Mantis (*Creobroter meleagris*). This hardy species will often perch on flowers or low-lying plants in wait for passing prey.

share very similar characteristics. *Theoprobus elegans,* the Orange Winged or Banded Flower Mantis from South East Asia, at first sight bears a striking resemblance to a number of the African *Creobroter* species. As its name suggests, it conceals a pair of particularly attractive tangerine coloured wings under its emerald green wing cases with cream eye spots. Members of the S. American genus *Acontista* also share this often confusing likeness.

   Creobroter meleagris, for which there is no common name other than 'African Flower Mantis', is one of several similar looking species of the genus *Creobroter* that share the same habitat requirements and are commonly available to the enthusiast. As is typical with most mantis species, the males are substantially more slender and the wings extend right over the abdomen whereas, in a well fed or gravid (pregnant) female, the abdomen is visible either side of the wings. Both species have small leafy projections on the legs, although the degree of specialisation falls a long way short of that of the Orchid Mantis.

   As a guide, most of these species can be kept in a similar fashion; in moderate humidity (70%) and at a temperature in the region of 75°F. It would be prudent to quiz the breeder or importer for more information concerning the exact requirements of the species in question.

Dead-Leaf Mantis (*Deroplatys sp. and Phyllocrania sp.*)
Many species of dead-leaf mantids are found in the tropics. As their name suggests,

they are often camouflaged as crumpled leaves and spend their time secreted among the foliage of trees and shrubs. This makes them very difficult to spot; even in a terrarium their resemblance to decaying leaves enables them to pass unnoticed to the untrained eye.

The Malaysian Dead-Leaf Mantis is readily available to the enthusiast from specialist suppliers and breeders.

Originating from Peninsular Malaysia, Borneo and Indonesia, *Deroplatys truncata, lobata* and *dessicata* are a mottled brown colour ranging from a pale orangey brown in some individuals right through to almost black, the majority of specimens encountered falling somewhere in between. All of these species exhibit considerable modification of the prothorax to a greater or lesser degree, so much so that in *D. dessicata* it has become paper thin, allowing light to shine through. A characteristic of these species is to hang upside down in clusters of leaves, rocking gently when disturbed as if they have been caught in a breeze. If the threat is greater they will hurl themselves off their perch and, holding their legs tightly to their body, they will fall to the forest floor where they will lie motionless, blending in perfectly with fallen leaves and thus avoiding detection. Another defensive ploy is to stand upright, extending the first pair of legs to either side and flashing their wings and the underside of their wing cases, which exhibit striking eye spots. This defence mechanism is also used by many other types of mantis.

Females are substantially larger and heavier than males which often look as if they should belong to another species. Such sexual dimorphism is a common characteristic of these mantids.

A species from Madagascar which is being bred with increasing regularity is *Phyllocrania paradoxa*. This is another remarkable leaf-mimic which, in the nymph form, resembles crumpled fern in various shades of gold, green, brown and black. With leafy projections covering the abdomen, legs and a large projection on the head the Madagascan Leaf Mantis is a real gem.

Although fragile in appearance, Dead-Leaf Mantids are surprisingly hardy subjects in captivity. The only real problem one is likely to encounter is during ecdysis when a previously healthy individual has difficulty in discarding its old skin, becoming tangled or trapped and emerging as a twisted cripple. This is one of the most upsetting aspects of mantis husbandry and is nearly always a result of unfavourable conditions - either incorrect humidity or the absence of a suitable perch from which to hang.

The two genera described have similar requirements: moderate humidity 70-80% and a temperature between 75-80°F. The terrarium can be decorated with artificial or real plants and a floor covering of peat or vermiculite will help maintain the desired level of humidity. Regular spraying is also important.

Egyptian Mantis (*Miomantis species*)

A small, slender species reaching only 3.5-4cm in length and assuming various shades of yellow, green and beige. The females are more heavily built but remain

Malaysian Dead-Leaf Mantis, male (*Deroplatys truncata*).

very slender and dainty. The male of the species is easily distinguished by its long antennae and is particularly active, bearing a passing resemblance to a form of lacewing. Both sexes fly well and, in their natural habitat, they are often attracted to outside lights in some numbers.

This is a short-lived species that is not difficult to maintain or breed and is therefore suited to the novice. Several specimens may be kept in the same terrarium providing there is ample space for retreat and they are well fed.

Other Mantis Species

This category could extend to innumerable pages. Fortunately for the beginner, many species can be maintained in much the same way and the rules for keeping one species can be applied to a great number providing that they originate from similar habitats.

African, European and Asian species tend to be the most commonly kept, with very few American representatives in culture. One European species that is commonly seen in the Mediterranean region, and sometimes encountered in captivity, is *Mantis religiosa* or the Common European Mantis. Reaching approximately 7.5-8 cm in length, this is a relatively slender species and is generally green or pale brown in colour. Care is the same as that for the African *Sphodromantis*.

Bizarre looking species belonging to the family Empusidae are occasionally available to the enthusiast. *Gongylus gongyloides* is one such oddity. This is a rare species found in India that possesses an extremely elongate prothorax and broad

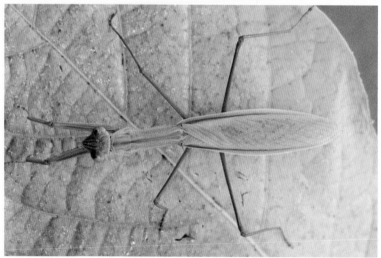

The Chinese Mantis (*Tenodera sinensis*). This is a large species capable of inflicting a painful bite if annoyed.

abdomen. Known locally as the 'Rose Insect', this mantis spends a large proportion of its time hiding among flowers and leaves. Apparently favouring rose bushes, its abdomen resembles the corolla of a flower. Although intriguing, this species is not recommended for the beginner as it is a sensitive subject to maintain, requiring a high temperature and quite specific environmental conditions in order to thrive.

Twig and stick mantids of the genus *Popa* make unusual additions to any collection. Closely resembling a bent twig, this small species is not difficult to care for and only requires a modest sized terrarium.

Other regularly encountered species are the Giant Chinese Mantis (*Tenodera aridifolia sinensis*) - a sizeable creature reaching almost 12cm in length - and members of the genus *Hierodula* which are widely distributed throughout Asia.

Indian Rose Mantis (*Gongylus gongyloides*). A convincing mimic of crumpled leaves, this attractive but delicate species is not for the beginner.

This sinister looking mantis is a member of the family Empusidae. A characteristic of this family is a slender stick-like appearance, often with feathery antennae. Photo: Sean Crawford

EQUIPMENT AND HOUSING

Very little in the way of specialist equipment is needed to keep and breed mantids successfully. They do not require elaborate set-ups and housing them can be achieved fairly inexpensively. Young nymphs can be adequately housed in a sweet

Perspex tanks with ventilated lids make perfectly satisfactory homes. Note the humidity meter and thermometer, useful aids when trying to regulate terrarium conditions.

jar or similar vessel with a net top. Larger individuals can be maintained in a small aquarium, perspex tank or purpose-built container.

The most important criteria for a mantis terrarium are height and ventilation; ground surface area is of lesser importance. Ideally, the terrarium should be a minimum of 30cm tall, 20cm deep and 20cm wide although these dimensions are not critical. A terrarium of these dimensions would comfortably house most adult mantids but the larger species may benefit from a more spacious enclosure.

A lid constructed from fine zinc mesh or netting, which is available from most hardware stores or entomological suppliers, is essential for two principle reasons. Firstly, to provide the necessary ventilation and, secondly, to provide the purchase required when a mantis needs to hang upside down to shed its skin. For these reasons the widely available and inexpensive perspex tanks with ventilated lids sometimes referred to as 'Pal pens' are ideal. When keeping a large number of

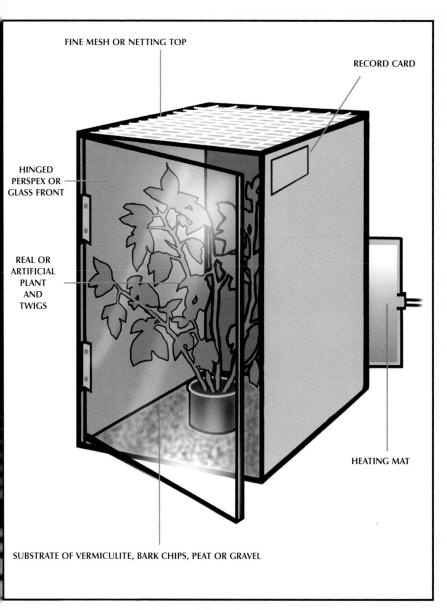

FINE MESH OR NETTING TOP

RECORD CARD

HINGED
PERSPEX OR
GLASS FRONT

REAL OR
ARTIFICIAL
PLANT
AND
TWIGS

HEATING MAT

SUBSTRATE OF VERMICULITE, BARK CHIPS, PEAT OR GRAVEL

A purpose built mantis enclosure.

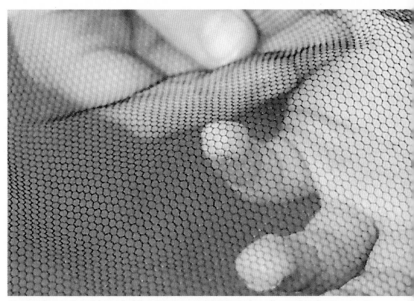

Fine netting such as this is ideal for covering rearing jars and can be used in the construction of net cages and other terraria.

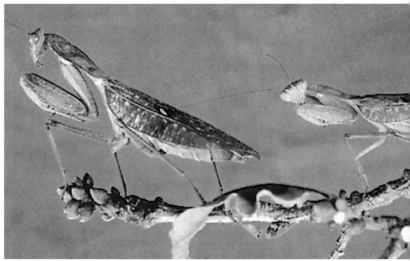

Prior to copulation, both mantids will engage in a battle of icy stares.
Photo: David Thomas

mantids, these containers can be easily stacked on top of one another and spraying can be carried out through the plastic grill lid.

Depending on the species being kept, the terrarium can be furnished with a variety of plastic, silk or real plants. Twigs and small pieces of driftwood can be incorporated into the layout to provide cover, perching material and to improve the aesthetics. With a little creativity quite a pleasing display can be achieved. However, it should be remembered that a cluttered terrarium will hinder the occupants' movement and could possibly obstruct the mantis when it is trying to shed its skin.

The floor covering can consist of bark chips, peat, gravel or vermiculite. The latter is a sterile mineral substance used mainly as a water holding agent in composts or as an insulation material. Invertebrate keepers have found this material to be of great value when keeping all manner of different creatures. It is light, sterile, holds a vast amount of water and is pleasing to the eye, lending itself well to use with mantids. Gravel or dry vermiculite is ideal for species living in desert or semi-arid environments but, for a more humid terrarium, peat, bark chips or damp vermiculite should be used. A useful addition to the terrarium is a hygrometer (humidity meter) to enable the keeper to maintain the correct level of humidity. A thermometer is, however, essential.

Many species of mantis will survive a British summer without any additional heating but in the winter supplementary warmth may be required. The most practical way of providing this heat is with the use of a low wattage heating mat or cable. Heating mats designed for use with reptiles emit a gentle warmth and can be fastened to the outside of one wall of the terrarium. A thermostat is not generally considered necessary with this type of heating but one should initially keep an eye on the terrarium temperature. Lighting is not particularly important for mantids - most species spend their lives in vegetation covered areas and sunlight is likely to be defused as a result. A windowsill is not a good place to position the mantis terrarium; apart from the risk of dangerously overheating, mantids often shy away from bright lights. As a rule, a glow as opposed to a glare is preferable and any source of illumination should be outside the terrarium to prevent the occupant from being burnt. Bright lighting will only serve to make the mantis even more secretive and the heat given off by incandescent light bulbs precludes their use.

Not all mantids should be handled; the larger species are able to bite and, although not dangerous, can draw blood.

Feeding

Mantids are typically a 'sit-and-wait' predator although some species do actively search for prey. As a result of this behaviour, meals are likely to be fairly infrequent. This is not usually a problem for the mantis because the very nature of its predatory strategy requires very little energy expenditure.

In captivity mantids need only be fed once or twice each week; young nymphs and gravid females require more regular meals and a large gravid female will consume crickets on a daily basis. Hatchling nymphs can be reared on micro-house crickets or fruitflies (the wingless variety are easier to handle) and, as the nymph grows, it can be tempted with correspondingly larger prey items.

Crickets and locusts form the staple diet of most captive mantids. Care should be taken when feeding locusts and bush crickets because they may be too powerful for the mantids and could injure them.

House crickets, silent crickets and hopper locusts are all suitable foods and can be purchased from most pet shops or are available mail-order. The mantis should be offered one or two items at a time (depending on the size of the item) and all uneaten foodstuffs should be removed. This prevents soiling of the terrarium and also avoids the risk of the prey item attacking the predator; for this reason black field crickets and adult locusts are not recommended as food. To facilitate the ease of handling, just before use the crickets can be placed in a sealed bag in the refrigerator; this will make them lethargic and thus easier to control.

The easiest and least time consuming method of feeding hatchling mantids is to place a complete culture of fruitflies in the terrarium. A hole can be cut into the lid of the culture container to regulate the release of the flies and the nymphs will feed whenever they are hungry. The provision of a constant supply of food enables the hatchling mantids to be reared en masse. This is the only practical way of rearing a large quantity of nymphs.

The abdomen of most mantis nymphs curls back over the body.

A recently imported mantis from Vietnam. Imported species are often in less than perfect
condition - hence the missing toes on one hind leg. Photo: David Thomas

Maintaining The Terrarium

Mantids are fastidiously clean creatures and spend a great deal of time running their
legs and antennae through their mouthparts. They produce very little in the way of
waste and, consequently, their terrarium rarely needs to be cleaned out. The
commonest form of contamination is in the form of discarded or partially eaten food
insects. If these are removed on a regular basis then the terrarium hardly needs to
be touched.

While a water dish is not necessary, regular spraying is. A houseplant sprayer can
be used to mist the terrarium and the droplets will satisfy the mantids' water
requirement at the same time as increasing the humidity. One should ensure that
the sprayer has not been used for anything other than water as insecticide residue,
for example, will obviously spell disaster!

As a rough guide, mantids originating from tropical rainforest environments
require a relative humidity in the region of 75-80% and a temperature in the high
70s(°F). Desert and semi-arid dwelling species would benefit from the moderately
low humidity of between 40% to 50%. Sub-tropical and temperate species fall
somewhere in between. It is useful to provide a temperature gradient as well as a
humidity gradient within the enclosure by positioning the heat source (if any) on one
wall and keeping one end of the tank slightly damper than the other.

Apart from regular (daily) spraying there is little else in the form of maintenance
that needs to be carried out.

Mantids spend a lot of time cleaning themselves.

Moulting

In common with all insects and any other invertebrates possessing a ridged exoskeleton, the only way a mantis can grow is by discarding its old, hardened skin or cuticle and moulting into a fresh, new, flexible one.

This process (known as ecdysis) is fascinating to observe. The mantis will hang upside down from a rough surface or twig by its back legs. Slowly, the old skin will split and a fragile 'new' insect will emerge. This is a critical time for the mantis as it will be defenceless and particularly vulnerable to attack. It may take an hour or so for the new skin to harden and the mantis should not be disturbed at this time. Crickets and other live foods may attack the mantis while it is moulting and it is for this reason that uneaten items should be removed immediately after feeding .

Every mantis will go through a series of moults before reaching adulthood. Each stage of development is known as an instar. With each successive moult there will be an increase in size; the wings and sexual organs will also develop but remain dysfunctional until the mantis reaches maturity. Adult mantids do not moult

Health Matters

A fit and healthy mantis will appear alert and cling firmly to the object on which it is standing. The abdomen should appear well rounded and be free of irregular bulges which may indicate the presence of an internal parasite, although this is generally only a problem with imported specimens.

It is a good idea to check that its toes (tarsi) are complete, especially on the hind legs where the tarsi are particularly important to the mantis when it hangs to moult. The legs should be strong and straight; bowed legs will be a sign of a previous problematic moult. The edges of the wings in adult mantids may become tattered, which can be used as a guide when determining age - a newly matured mantis will appear perfect. Older and wild-caught mantids often look a little on the tatty side. If it is a wild-caught female then it is possible mating has already taken place, so its external appearance may not be such an important consideration if one intends to raise another generation. However, a tatty looking male mantis should be avoided as it is likely to be nearing the end of its lifespan.

If a mantis refuses to feed, it could indicate a number of things. Firstly, it could be approaching a moult, in which case there is no reason for concern. Secondly, it may suggest that the temperature of the terrarium is too low, especially if the mantis appears sluggish. Thirdly, and most disappointingly, its reluctance to feed may mean that the mantis is winding down prior to death. In all instances an alternative food should be offered; maybe the food items are unpalatable, too large or too small for the mantis to cope with and a change of diet could stimulate feeding.

Mantids rarely suffer from mites or other external parasites. Should a terrarium become infested the solution is a thorough clean out and replacement of the decor. Under no circumstances should insecticide sprays or treatments be used.

BREEDING AND REARING

For a long time it was thought that the female decapitated the male during copulation to improve the male's vigour. While this 'fact' ensured the mantis a place in the insect hall of fame, the reality is that this observation was based on a small captive sample and is largely inaccurate. The female will sometimes attack the male and fatalities can occur. As in the courtship of many invertebrate species, mating can be a risky business.

It is now widely accepted that chemical messages or pheromones released by the receptive female play an important part in attracting a mate. This is especially true of the cryptic leaf and flower mimicking species where their camouflage not only conceals them from predators but also potential mates. Because these pheromones are only released for a very short period of time, often in the early hours of the morning, the time at which mantids are paired is critical.

Before breeding is attempted ensure that you have two mature individuals of the same species. This may seem an obvious point but due to the considerable sexual dimorphism (differences) exhibited in some species they may be incorrectly identified. Sexing mantids is not always a straightforward affair. Small nymphs of certain species are notoriously difficult to sex; even with the aid of a magnifying glass, 100% accuracy cannot be guaranteed. Adults, on the other hand, often exhibit quite significant differences between the sexes, so much so that they could easily be mistaken for being different species. Males are typically smaller, more slender and sometimes possess longer antennae. Males invariably mature in advance of the females and this can be a useful guide when rearing a group of nymphs from the same batch. However, the most accurate way of sexing is by comparing the underside of the abdomen. Females have six visible segments and males typically have seven or sometimes more, depending on the species. Sexing is easiest when the abdomen is fully distended after a large meal.

Having found a suitable pair, ideally young adults, they should be well fed prior to introduction. The male can be placed in the female's terrarium or in a neutral pairing tank while the female is distracted by a strategically timed meal. Both individuals will freeze and lock in a battle of penetrating stares. If all goes well, the male will mount the female and copulation will take place. This can be a lengthy process and may last several hours. Following copulation the male should be removed. In about 28 days time an ootheca will be produced; if the mating was successful it will be fertile and will typically hatch in another three or four weeks. The ootheca consists of an arrangement of eggs protected by a foamy mass which quickly hardens to provide a protective coating. Its shape and size varies considerably among species and it will be attached to any suitable hard surface - often a terrarium wall or branch. The female will produce ootheca even if she has not been mated but these will be infertile.

Several fertile egg masses can be produced from one successful mating due to the mantid's ability to store sperm. The hatchling nymphs will erupt from the ootheca, suspended on fine threads. They will immediately moult and fall to the ground and often remain in close proximity to the ootheca for several days. Female mantids will invariably remain with the ootheca during incubation and keep a watchful eye on the nymphs after hatching.

Many hundreds of nymphs can emerge from one ootheca but only a fraction of those will survive to adulthood. Rearing nymphs can present a bit of a challenge to the novice and one has to accept the fact that many will perish. The most satisfactory way of rearing is to suspend the unhatched ootheca in a net cage which is in turn placed in a glass or plastic terrarium. The netting will provide a large area from which the nymphs can hang and the glass tank will allow the correct level of humidity and temperature to be maintained. Hatchling nymphs often have a habit of drowning in condensation; by using this method the problem is avoided. The nymphs can be reared en masse and separated into individual quarters as they grow. Providing there is a readily available supply of food (see the basic care section), cannibalism should not result in too many fatalities.

USEFUL ADDRESSES

Cicada Biological Supply
White Leaved Oak
Bromsberrow
Ledbury
Herefordshire
HR8 1SE
(For general entomological supplies, foods, books and livestock)

Watkins & Doncaster
Conghurst Lane
Four Thorns
Hawkhurst
Kent
TN18 5ED
(For preserving fluids, books and natural history supplies)

The Amateur Entomological Society
PO Box 8774
London
SW7 5ZG

Pet Reptile Magazine
Alexander House
Tower Park
Ling Road
Portsmouth
Hants
(A monthly publication covering invertebrates, reptiles and amphibians)